I Am Not Happy with Your Behaviour!

By Jacquie Kaufman

HUMMINGBIRD PUBLISHING

I Am Not Happy with Your Behaviour! Copyright © 2021 by Jacquie Kaufman. All rights reserved. No part of this book may be used or reproduced in any manner whatsoever without written permission except in the case of brief quotations in the context of critical articles or reviews.

ISBN 978-1-7774834-0-1

Cover and interior design by Aaxel Author Services
& VeeVee Creative Studio

To all my children, who became my teachers.

Table of Contents

What an Educator/Parent Needs to Know 4

The Strategy 16

Scenarios 23
    - Ages 16 months to 23 months 23
    - Ages 2 years to 3 years 30
    - Ages 3 years to 4 years 36
    - Ages 4 years to 5 years 39

Summary 46

Conclusion 47

Has This Ever Happened to You?

You are sitting in a restaurant having a peaceful meal with your family and over at the next table, there is a young family of four: a little girl who seems to be about four-and-a-half years old, a young infant, and mom and dad. The little girl is being disruptive; she has finished eating and is fidgeting in her chair, playing with anything she can find around her. The dad is talking on his phone, and the mom is busy with the baby. All of a sudden, you hear the dad loudly ask his daughter, "Can't you just sit still?" Then she begins to cry, and the mother suggests that she leave the table with the little girl to look at a showcase which features a collection of antique dolls. The little girl goes, but she is now in the way of the servers, who are carrying hot food.

Where is the joy in this family outing? What's happening in this situation? Is there a method to raise children who are happy, well-adjusted and a pleasure to be around?

These are very reachable goals, but success does not come without a lot of effort on the adults' part. We must remember that children from birth to age 25 are not adults or little adults, no matter how smart, precocious, and independent they may appear. Young children make decisions by acting on their emotional impulses. As they age, logical thought develops and becomes more important in the decision-making process. We cannot assume that the thought processes of anyone under age 25 are the same as an adult. It's wise to remember that we are all unique, and our development occurs in a personal fashion and on a unique time schedule.

This handbook is based on my many years of experience. I'm a mother of three successful adults, and I've been an educator for over 40 years, teaching children from the ages of 18 months to five years old. I am also a professor at private Colleges in Montreal, Quebec. I have been involved in the education of children 0-12 years old as well and I am a lecturer to educators in the field of childhood education at various daycares and professional conferences.

As a professor and supervisor to student teachers, I have noticed that not only do parents have difficulty managing their children's disruptive behaviour, but at times, so do teachers. Through intense observations in various situations, I have come to the conclusion that adults today are not truly respecting our children. We aren't really listening, or watching their behaviour. A child's behaviour is a form of communication, and adults should be making more of an effort to become aware of what children are telling us through their actions.

We can't expect a three year old to turn to a parent and say, "Can you get off your phone and pay attention to me?" However, if this child starts to act out, then the parent automatically shifts their attention to the child. Then the child is successfully getting what they want and need: "attention". Unfortunately, this is negative attention, but the child is still being recognized.

We should always consider the child's behaviour as a form of communication. They are telling us something. Therefore, if we become observant of our child's moods and actions, we will be better able to understand and fulfill their needs in a positive way. We will also be able to enjoy our children more, and not have to worry about disruptive behaviour that can manifest when a child feels bored, lonely, neglected or ignored.

This handbook will discuss the strategy of "choice." I have found that when a child is offered a choice, many developmental skills are encouraged. This strategy engages the child to become responsible for his own behavior that is socially acceptable.

What An Educator/ Parent Needs to Know

Before we get started:

When discussing the development of socially acceptable behaviour, there's a lot of background knowledge a caregiver should have:

- A personal philosophy is a tool that the educator/parent should think about, as it will be the basis of her attitude and interactions with not only the children in her care, but also how the children relate to others in their world.

- The educator should also have skills to enable her to relate to the needs of the children. As a parent, these skills are also helpful to navigate the complicated world of child development.

- The educator should also have concrete knowledge of child development to be able to care for the children in a positive and appropriate manner. This knowledge should be obtained by attending certified educational institutions.

Author's Philosophy

<u>**The 3 R's:**</u>

From my experience, I have created a philosophy that allows me to enjoy my children, grandchildren and students. I basically live and teach with a philosophy of the 3R's: **R**ESPECT, **R**ESPONSIBILITY and **R**EALISTIC EXPECTATIONS.

Respect

I was raised to show respect to all people, to listen when someone is talking, not to throw garbage out a car window, and not to use offensive words. It seems that today we have forgotten how to show basic respect for the people and the environment around us. But what *is* respect? I believe that it means being mindful of others, and thinking about the effect of your personal actions. Respect is also acceptance of the uniqueness of all people, recognizing that "different" is a good quality to have and be.

Responsibility

Have you been in a situation where someone has made an innocent mistake but does not admit to it, and at times blames another person for their error? Why does that happen? And how can we teach children that it's *okay* to make a mistake? In fact, it's essential to remind children not to strive for perfection. We all learn from our mistakes and it's an important life skill to be able to use them in our growth and development.

Realistic Expectations

At times we expect more from ourselves and also from our children than is possible or attainable. We also tend to forget about age-appropriate abilities. A two-year-old boy is not physically capable of totally dressing himself, but he *is* capable of helping the adult dress him. If we ask too much from a child, then, we inevitably set him up for failure. But if we do not challenge the child and do everything for him, then, we tell him through our behaviour that we feel he is not capable of being independent or autonomous.

It's amazing the reaction I get when I use the 3 R's in my day-to-day dealings with people. All of a sudden, they feel more relaxed, and therefore, they become kind and helpful. They also hear the respect in my tone of voice, since it is nonjudgmental and not threatening. I believe that all children are born kind and good; they just need a chance to relax, enjoy their lives, and be respected.

Although this book's focus is on childhood behaviour, adult behaviour is almost always the catalyst for a child's behaviour. The way adults react to a child's behaviour has a direct effect on the child's disposition, mood, and at times, temperament. (Let's also note that most adults also react in the same way.) I feel the main reason why these 3 R's work is because we are rewarding a person with a positive attitude with attention. Showing respect changes behaviour in both children, and adults.

Attention

According to the research into human development (especially Abraham Maslow and Eric Erickson, (www.simplypsychology.org)), it has been shown that people have basic needs that must be fulfilled in order to become well-adjusted adults. These needs must also be met in the proper order of our stages of growth and development in order for our children to grow and develop successfully. It's only with the guidance of adults, our culture, and environment that they will develop into healthy adults.

To help us meet these needs, the 3 R's should be used by parents and educators in our daily interactions with children. In order for our children to develop into productive adults, we must provide the basic needs of security, respect, in loving and comforting environments, children must feel that they are important and worthy of their existence, (Bowlby theory of attachment)

But we must not forget to always recognize that the behaviours of the child teach us what each individual one needs. Each child is unique, and therefore has specific needs that only an adult can fulfill to guarantee appropriate development. Note that the child will seek out fulfillment of his own personal needs. It is always better if an adult is available to help guide the child to achieve this goal, ensuring that their needs are fulfilled in a socially acceptable way

We are all born with a basic desire to receive attention. A child is also born with the ability to scream, and to fill their lungs with air. We should interpret this scream as a way of telling us, "I am here; pay attention to me!"

Adults also desire to be recognized, preferably by positive acknowledgement of work that is well done. They have control of their behaviours, and usually display only those that will get them the attention they want. Children are not able to control their actions in the same rational way as an adult hence their reactions and actions are impulses. Their impulse control is developing, and keeps developing up to the age of 25.

It is crucial that children be acknowledged, since their social and emotional—and at times cognitive—development depends on how they are treated by their significant adults. Unfortunately, we tend not to notice the good behaviours, and only observe and give voice to the inappropriate ones. It brings to mind the old expression, "The squeaky wheel gets the grease."

Isn't this what we are currently doing to our children? We must train ourselves to be observant of the child who plays cooperatively and respectfully with others, shows initiative, and seems to enjoy learning and being in the classroom environment. We also have to recognize these children and praise them so that they can feel important and continue to develop in a healthy and happy way.

This is how we promote strong self-esteem and a concept of the self. Children want to please and be accepted by the significant adults in their life. If we ignore these subtle, positive behaviours, we are indirectly telling the child that he is not seen and not making any impact on our lives. Then there is a good chance that this child will now notice the misbehaving child, who gets all our attention, and then starts to copy that child's behaviours.

When we show all children that they are important to us, acknowledging their *good* behaviours and giving them time and attention, we are showing them that *"respectable behaviours" receive attention.* Eventually, almost all children will follow this pattern. While I'm referring here to the educator in a classroom, this application is very appropriate for parents, too.

There is no limit to the amount of attention we can give a child, but we must always be honest, sincere, and consistent with our praise. If we are not, this deception will be easily detected, and all of our good intentions will become not only ineffective, but also harmful.

We must also be consistent with our consequences when safety rules are not followed, or if a behaviour is dangerous to the child, or to others around them. A child should always feel physically safe and not mentally stressed, so that they can be calm and enjoy themselves while learning and playing. When a child is happy and well-behaved, the adult caregiver shows less stress and therefore is also calm and positive.

We must realize that this relationship is reciprocal. In other words, since we are social beings, our moods and behaviours are reflective of other people, and affect them, as well.

I believe one cannot change a person's nature, but we *can* change our reactions to their nature and behaviour.

Skills

Children need the tools and skills to navigate the often complex road to adulthood. It's imperative that adults and caregivers possess excellent skills in the following areas to be successful developmental guides for our children's journeys.

- **Observation skills**

    This is when teachers and caregivers learn the individual needs of the child. This gathering of information is done through a process of collecting data in an unbiased and authentic way. Observation is more than just noticing what a child (or groups of children) is doing, it is a focused reporting in which information is collected and analyzed by the caregiver to help identify the needs of the child. No assumptions are made, nor predictions. This collection of information is shared with other professionals and parents, the child's stage of development is determined and their strengths and weaknesses are examined. This will enable the parent and caregiver to plan and design activities to promote development in social, emotional, cognitive and physical domains.

- **Social skills that enable us to build meaningful relationships**

    When children and their teachers are in a comfortable relationship with each other, the true personal traits of the child emerge. Research shows us that relaxed children are eager to learn and explore their world. When there are positive interactions between a child and caregiver, questions, ideas and knowledge flow freely.

- **Communication skills: respect for oneself and others**

    Having good communication skills enables the teacher and caregiver to succeed in building meaningful relationships, not only with the child, but also with parents and colleagues. Good relations promote the opportunity to learn from others and therefore, increase our personal knowledge. These positive relationships create pleasant and relatively stress-free environments. When everyone is happy, they are eager to become important team members and work to their capacity for the betterment of not only themselves, but also of their team.

- **Listening skills**

    When a teacher and caregiver have good listening skills, they are showing respect to the child and enhancing her self-esteem. They can learn a lot about the child while she is talking and playing, with this knowledge the child's development and creativity can grow in a positive way. When we are open to each other's ideas, thoughts and experiences, we reach new dimensions in our personal development.

- **Organization skills**

    If we aren't organized when it comes to all the information collected in our observations, this important knowledge may get lost and not be utilized to its full potential. Throughout the day, the teacher and caregiver must be constantly aware of the children in their care. This includes the safety and appropriateness of the environment, so they can plan activities that will be beneficial to each child.

If the teacher and caregiver don't know the supplies in their room, neither the goals nor objectives that have decided upon based on the all the skills learned above, will be attained. The teacher will become ineffective and burn out. Note that everyone is unique and therefore, we all have our own organization styles, but if the environment is home to more than one caregiver, then a certain style must be agreed upon by all parties in order to achieve success in a calm environment.(it is very hard to bake a cake if a main ingredient is missing!)

For educators and parents to be able to fulfill the needs of a child, they must listen, talk, interact and build meaningful relationships with them, so that they can get to know the child individually. All human beings are unique (no matter their age), and therefore, each of us has our own strengths, weaknesses, likes, and dislikes. To best promote self-esteem and a strong concept of self, it is imperative that we first take the time to observe all that the child does, know what they like and dislike, and learn their natural strengths.

Behaviours are an important key that reveal many aspects of the personality and temperament of the child. Although part of this is genetic, life experiences can also affect a person's disposition and outlook—as well as their behaviour. It's vital that our observations are done both with direct contact with the child, and also indirectly. It's also extremely important that our interpretations of our observations are unbiased and without prejudice. Since we live in diverse communities, we must also learn about the child's culture and norms.

We can learn a lot about a child when we watch them interact with others, play with their toys, talk with their friends and engage in solitary activities. When we connect with and observe children, we can analyze their behaviours, but we are also indirectly giving them attention and making them feel important. Since we now have knowledge of the child and the group of children through this constant interaction, we are able to plan activities that are interesting and engaging to them. We are making the child feel that they are important, not only to us, but to others as well. We are also helping the child develop a positive attitude about herself, which will help her become a successful adult.

When we show empathy and give support to children in our care, we are teaching them to do the same to others. Children also learn by observation and imitation; therefore, the child who sees and lives with positive role models will begin to imitate these behaviours and become a positive member of a group. They will also accept challenges more readily in social and academic situations, because this child will have a healthy concept of self and strong self-esteem. These feelings of positive self-worth will equip the child with the necessary tools to help deflect any type of bullying. Thus, this child will make good decisions and good behaviour choices.

Children react positively when they feel that they are important. By making the effort to not only observe behaviours, but also listen and interpret the behaviour, we are actively showing the child that they are important and deserving of our attention.

Parenting/Teaching Styles

Different parenting/teaching styles:

- **Authoritarian style:**

    This is when the adult takes all responsibility in the determination of every aspect of the child's life. Every decision involving the child is made with almost no discussion with the child. The child must follow the adult's directives without questioning or challenging anything. We often associate this style with the "children are here to only be seen and not heard" mentality.

- **Authoritative style:**

    This style involves not only the parent, but the child as well, when it comes to determining the child's development. The parent consults the child and listens to the child. The child has an important role in the decisions, and this will help him develop into a successful adult. His interests, likes and dislikes are taken into consideration when decisions have to be made. The child is shown respect and is encouraged to talk and contribute to the discussions that refer to him. This is a cooperative style of parenting between the parent and child.

- **Permissive style:**

    This style is the opposite of the Authoritative style. It basically involves the child making all the decisions about his well-being. The parent does not assert her adult viewpoint nor excise her parental obligations in the promotion of her child's development. Bedtime, mealtimes and all other important decisions involving the welfare of the child are left up to the child. The parent is involved in the child's life as the child suggests different options, but ultimately leaves the final decisions to the child. The parent ensures that the child is safe, fed, clothed and feels loved, but allows the child to make the important decisions, with very little adult input.

- **Neglectful style:**
  This style completely removes the parent from participating in the child's development. The parent essentially gives the responsibility to another person. She ensures that the basic needs are met by this other caregiver and only wants to be kept updated on the child's progress. This parent is involved with the child only on a superficial level. The child and caregiver are basically left to their own devices. The caregiver makes all decisions for the child and informs the parent when necessary. The parent and child are not involved with each other on a daily basis.

Parenting styles are parallel to teaching styles

These are basic definitions of the different parenting styles available and most often, a combination of them is appropriate for the benefit of the child. A parenting/teaching style is very personal and each caregiver should self-reflect in order to incorporate their personality into their parenting and teaching styles.

I believe that it's the obligation of the child's caregiver/parent to promote their child's development, be involved in all aspects of their care and to nurture the child, thus enabling the child to grow and develop into a secure adult. This is an ever-changing and difficult job, but the end results make it worthwhile. There are many other aspects of child development, and the next chapters will further explain how to ensure that your child grows into a confident adult.

The Strategy

Teaching a child to not only make good decisions, but also to become responsible for their decisions, is another important skill that adults should focus on. The earlier we give a child the chance to make a decision, the more we promote human development and autonomy. Making a decision involves the cognitive domain (thinking), as well as the emotional and social domains of child development. The more we encourage the child in decision-making, the better the child's skills will be in their future development.

As teachers and parents, we must make sure that the decision we are asking the child to make or the choice we are giving him is age appropriate and socially acceptable. When giving a child a choice between two options, we must ensure that they include what we want for the child, while also incorporating the child's interests, desires and needs.

For example, if it's the child's bedtime and he does not want to go to bed, the decision-making process begins. We can ask the child the following:

a) Would he like to go to bed by himself?

or

b) Would he like the caregiver to go with him?

In giving these two choices to the child, the reality of bedtime is not part of the decision. Instead, the decision revolves around *how* the child is going to go to bed. Whatever decision the child makes, it is an appropriate one. Thus, the child feels that he has some control over the situation and feels respected.

Being respected promotes self-esteem and enhances a positive self-image. The child feels important because he feels that he has been listened to and is actively involved in his own development. Therefore, the responsibility of not only the behaviour—but also the decision—is the child's. And since only acceptable choices are given, there should not be any opportunity for unacceptable behaviour.

If afterwards the child wants to change his decision, it should not be an option. The child should be reminded that he made his choice this time, and that next time, he can change his decision. It's acceptable to change the decision at a different time, but we must teach the child to take responsibly for his own decisions. It is up to the child—with the help of the adult—to make the decision work.

As soon as a child is capable of making a choice, we can incorporate it as a decision-making tool. An infant as young as six months makes decisions all the time, although they are making them as impulsive actions. We can show her two different toys, and she will choose one to play with (for a few seconds). As the infant grows and develops, their decisions and choices become more complex, challenging and age appropriate.

No matter what age, the act of decision-making has great implications on a child's future behaviour and happiness.

We must not forget, however, that there are times when decision-making or giving choices to the child are not appropriate. Sometimes, the adult has to take control of a situation and make fast decisions for the child. When the safety of the child is involved, the adult must take immediate action to ensure that the child keeps out of harm's way. "No" is an acceptable word, but should be used only when appropriate. If the child is constantly told "no," this word quickly loses its power, and at worse, becomes ignored.

I AM NOT HAPPY WITH YOUR BEHAVIOUR!

When a child is repeatedly being given negative directives, these comments hinder positive growth and delay development. For example, when a child around 18 months is starting to become verbal and is corrected by an adult on their pronunciation, grammar or the proper use of new words, this child will become fearful to explore new ones, and their potential development of a broad vocabulary becomes unlikely. The challenge and joy of experimentation has not been encouraged in this scenario, and therefore, the child retreats to a place where positive reinforcement *is* given.

If a child comes from a culture that does not encourage children to speak in public (or talk with adults), she will learn this and may not talk to express her thoughts. We must always remember that a child idolizes the adults in her life, and therefore needs and seeks their attention, recognition, affection and praise.

We should also make sure that this attention is positive and promotes healthy development, not only in the cognitive domain, but also in the emotional realms of development. I strongly believe that children are able to develop a strong sense of self and good self-esteem, given the chance. I also believe that most parents may not realize the negative impact they can have on a child's emotional well-being.

Professional caregivers and educators must always be aware of their impact on the children in their care. An educator is not only responsible for the whole child's development, but she must also respectfully engage the parent throughout this process. Parents may know their children best, but they might not realize what their role is, and how best to help their child develop to their full potential.

Expectations change from generation to generation and from culture to culture. Child development must be promoted to encompass all these changes. However, as educators, we are obliged to look after the whole child so that they will have the tools and skills to become a successful adult.

Parents should appreciate the educator's knowledge, the change of expectations due to technology advancement, and the impact of changing cultures in our society, including the mixing of different ethnicities that our children now experience. Change is all around, and all of us must have the skills to adapt.

Parents tend to parent their children as they were parented. They look at their own childhood background to help them establish a parenting style. This can happen with educators too, but when new knowledge about child development emerges, we must be aware of our bias, remain open to this research and use it as a tool to aid a child's growth.

If an adult was raised by a particular parenting style that did not promote personal autonomy, the parenting skills passed down in that environment will probably not help the child acquire the proper skills needed for success in the future. It's my opinion that this healthy development, which encompasses modern standards, must include the parent *and* have cultural input.

We must also acknowledge the parent, culture and environment as equally important factors to accomplish our goal of raising a child into a self-sufficient adult. Therefore, the parent has the responsibility to give their child the most healthy and positive home life, while at the same time encouraging the involvement of the educator.

The educator must also become a role model, and give guidance to the parent so that the parent can acquire useful skills to implement.

There are many parenting styles to choose from, and the style that a parent uses may be based on his culture, memory of his childhood, or society's influences of the day. According to the theories of Uri Bronfenbrenner, a child learning theorist, children's development is greatly influenced by not only their family's values and circumstances, but also by the culture and values that they are surrounded by. Our North American culture has a very different philosophy on child rearing than many other parts of the world. This book will not discuss these other philosophies, but we must be aware that there are some basic principles of development that should be addressed in order for a child to grow up to become a functioning member of society.

A trained professional must constantly appreciate that what the child learns in his home environment is reflected in his behaviours away from home. An environment that is safe and secure will enable the child to develop appropriately. The educator must also have good observation skills, so that the needs of the child are not only met, but also challenged.

Choice...
A Magic Word!

Choice is a strategy that helps develop positive behaviours and build important skills to ensure that a child evolves into a productive adult in society. It is a two-part strategy that involves both the adult caregiver and the child. Each participant makes a choice as to which actions are best suited to the scenario for it to have a positive conclusion. The adult decides what the goals to achieve in the situation are and then guides the child to find a resolution, by giving the child choices that will lead to a successful outcome. This feeling of success builds self-esteem.

When a person feels autonomous, it creates a strong sense of self and enhances self-esteem. This philosophy of having children take responsibility for their behaviours is based on choices. The adult routinely offers alternatives (choices) to the child and thus the process begins, leading to much growth and positive development.

One way to learn how to make a choice is by imitating someone else or role modeling. According to research, human beings are not born knowing or understanding the concept of sharing. So, when a toddler sees her parents sharing, communicating and helping each other at home, this behaviour will usually be imitated.

Below are age-related scenarios that show the process of implementing the 3 R's, using *choice* as the main tool:

The 3 R's:

- **Respect**

    A child will respond to an adult who is genuine and caring, and when given choices of how to act in a situation, they will accept the guidance of this trusted adult.

- **Responsibility**

    We should always encourage the child to be responsible for their actions. This will promote healthy self-esteem, a strong sense of identity and improved self-confidence.

- **Realistic Expectations**

    The choices that are given to the child should be appropriate to the child's abilities.

Scenarios

Ages 16 months to 23 months:

At this age, the child is considered a toddler who is just beginning to be physically and cognitively able to control their impulses and actions. With this emerging ability of impulse-control, the toddler, under the guidance of a caring adult, will become a caring child. As research has proven time and time again, children learn from observing and imitating.

They are becoming mobile and with this ability comes freedom and independence. They are also acquiring language and with the skill of verbal communication comes the ability to express their needs and desires. This language acquisition is developing at a rapid rate.

This is the time in a child's development when the significant adult plays a very crucial role. If the adults in the child's life are attentive, nurturing and realize they are meant to be positive role models; the child's overall development will be strong and joyful.

Remember: Toddlers are just beginning to develop a sense of themselves, their importance, their feelings and their likes and dislikes. They are also realizing that they have an impact on the world they live in. The people they interact with can either impede their progress or promote their development. We must also realize that a basic tool of learning for anyone is imitation, so being a good role model is also being an effective teacher.

Here is an example of role modelling, a how it affects child development. We humans are not born knowing or understanding the concept of sharing (Maslow's hierarchy of needs). If a toddler sees her parents sharing, communicating, and helping each other at home, this behaviour will be imitated.

We just have to watch a toddler play with her dolls, cars, or other toys, and then we can see exactly what the child has experienced. If the child is gentle and caring toward the doll and allows others to be involved in the play, we are safe to assume that this child has observed similar experiences.

If the child shows some anger or resentment, it is imperative for the caregiver to seek out the reasons for this behaviour. When we see a negative attitude and just shout at the child or display other negative responses, we are only perpetuating the negative.

A toddler is also learning how to control her impulses with the guidance and modeling of the adult, who is showing the child personal control. Sharing and caring for others will show the child the desired behaviour through observation. They will then learn these skills and develop into an empathic child.

Scenario 1

Your toddler refuses to get dressed in the morning, and you are rushing to drop her off at daycare and get to work on time. This has become a consistent issue.

These are the choices:

a. Let the child go to daycare in their pajamas.

b. Dress the child against their will during an extremely stressful experience that will certainly continue at the breakfast table and possibly throughout the morning.

c. Turn this negative experience into a positive lesson and take the opportunity to enhance the child's self-esteem.

Consequences of your decision:

a. This choice may put the child in a situation where he may be ridiculed by classmates, leading him to dress appropriately the next day. But this experience may be so devastating that it will have a negative effect on his emotional development. So, no skills are developed here, just negative emotions.

b. This choice leads to a power struggle where the child usually wins as the adult gives up because of the realities of life. If this behaviour is ongoing, then it has become not only a pattern but also a constant power struggle. Remember that the child's concept of self is starting to emerge now, and with this development comes the child's knowledge of her power when she says "no" to the parent. The adult shouldn't get involved in any power struggle, because usually the child wins, reinforcing the negative behaviour and encouraging it to be applied in many other situations that the child may want to control. Children at this age lack the cognitive ability to "Control "but are being directed by impulses and emotional needs. The adult allows this false control by giving in to tantrums and all unacceptable behaviors, usually because the adult is in a time crunch!

    c. You might wonder how this third choice can be accomplished in the short time available during this morning ritual.

Giving the child a choice diffuses the power struggle and allows for a calm and productive resolution. It is best to have a relaxing exchange with child in order to establish a new routine for the morning dressing. Since it has been established that this behaviour has become a pattern, then the getting-dressed routine should start the previous evening, just before bedtime, if that is not also a stressful time. If it is, pick a calm time instead to preplan!

The adult should organize the child's closet and drawers to display only daycare-appropriate clothing. Then the adult asks the child to choose two outfits that she thinks she may like to wear after she wakes up. In the morning, the child then chooses her outfit to wear to school and starts to dress herself!

Why does the element of choice work? Firstly, the power struggle is immediately eliminated and the child feels the respect from the adult by being given a role in an important decision. She also feels proactive in this important routine, her sense of self is encouraged and she feels successful! The adult is not stressed with the child's decision of what to wear because she has previously removed any inappropriate choices. Notice there is no negativity or stress in this experience. The adult can now praise the child and the child feels very positive about herself.

Next, breakfast can be enjoyed in a calm atmosphere!

This example works in many different scenarios and with all ages (even with difficult teens and adults).

By observing the child's behaviour, you see past the negative experience. You must acknowledge that the child is seeking recognition, and by acting out, she is successfully receiving it. When you change the situation and realize that the responsibility of choosing the outfit gives positive attention to the child, you now have a content child who feels good about herself and those around her.

This feeling will only last until the next power-struggle altercation, however. Be prepared for many other ones! Although a child at this age is developing memory, it is still mostly an emotional memory. It's important to remember that memory development and retention is greatly enhanced by repeated experiences.

At this age, the child is becoming aware of her effect on adults, other children and her environment. Sometimes her behaviour stems from exploratory curiosity. Whatever the reason for the socially unacceptable behaviour, however, the adult must address it.

Scenario 2

A 20-month-old child is playing with a toy at daycare. Another child comes and grabs the toy away, and the first child starts to cry. She is close enough to grab the toy back, however with a very strong push, the other child falls. The educator now has two crying toddlers!

These are the choices:

a. The educator puts both children in a time-out.

b. The educator runs to the child that has fallen over and berates the other for pushing her.

c. The educator waits and watches to see what happens. She then guides the children to share the toy and show concern for the one who may be hurt.

Consequences of your decision:

a. This choice does not provide any role modeling or guidance to help the children discover their own solutions to their problems. Their feelings are not being acknowledged or addressed, and therefore, respect is lacking.

b. Again, the teacher is taking control of the situation, but not really addressing any of the underlying issues. The children are being judged because of the consequence that they are both crying. It is not really known which child started this altercation. We're told that one child grabbed a toy, but which child had the toy first? Does this child always take toys from others, or is this a first-time behaviour? Remember, it is important to know the whole story before punishing a child.

c. The educator calmly walks over to the two children, assesses the situation calmly, makes sure that no one is hurt, and then takes the hands of both children to help them negotiate a solution, providing them with the necessary words to express their feelings.

After the children are calm, the educator can give the children possible choices that will resolve the conflict. Equal time should be given to each child to be a part of the happy resolution.

The educator then provides positive alternatives to the children so that the toy can be shared amicably. The role of the educator here is to explain and demonstrate the proper behaviour in language that the children will understand. Using puppets, hand-play stories, or just simple explanations will work.

Then the children should be given a choice of which toy to play with, and also be encouraged to play together. The children should be left to play under the watchful eye of the educator. This process takes longer to explain than to do! It also has to be repeated many times to children of this age, so that they can absorb, understand, and remember when and how to resolve events themselves. This is a learning process, after all.

It can also work in the home with siblings and parents. The key to success is to always remember that the adult is in charge, not the child. The use of choice can be instigated by the adult, but it must be done very quickly in order to achieve a positive outcome. The final decision must always be encouraged by the adult. The adult must also remember to consistently praise the child for their good choices and behaviour. This is key to building good self-esteem and a strong concept of self.

Although we are discussing a young child in this example, the foundation to being a successful adult actually starts at this age—and even younger! If the child is recognized for their positive attributes, it is natural that they will use 'good behaviour' to receive the attention that they need.

If the child receives very little praise and more negative reactions from their significant adult, they will seek out more negative methods that will fulfill their prime need for attention. Happily, this cycle of undesirable behaviour can be reversed!

Ages 2 years to 3 years:

We have all heard about the "terrible twos"- and it's true that this is a very exciting and trying growth period for children (and parents)!

Physical development is rapid at this point, and the child is becoming very comfortable in the upright position. Running, walking backwards, hopping on two feet, negotiating steps, and dancing are all being explored.

What does this development mean for the teacher and parent? Since we know that the child is moving, we must make his environment safe, yet also interesting and challenging. We want to encourage this physical development, after all, not inhibit it.

At this time, the small muscles of the child are also getting stronger, and he is showing more control over his movements. He is touching and picking up medium-sized objects, using his hands as tools, and starting to coordinate his movements. For example, he can now use forks and spoons to eat completely by himself, and even pour liquids into cups.

Language at this age is exploding, and with this development comes the ability of the child to express their needs, interests and feelings. Now the toddler can both understand and adapt to others in a simplistic way. Their world is still a place where they are integral, but we also see them starting to find room for others in it as well. In other words, the child is becoming more social, wanting to be with others and to be included in various experiences with people of all sorts of different ages.

Socialization is fundamental, and therefore it is very important for caregivers to be good role models. At this age, we see individual characters forming, but remember that a lot of values and behaviour from these children are still coming from imitating others.

Children now are also exhibiting knowledge of what makes them happy and sad. We see them becoming increasingly frustrated when they are not understood or acknowledged. This is when they will assert themselves to get what they want—in whichever way will be successful in getting the attention of the adult.

Once we know the needs of this age group, we are able to adapt the environment and curriculum program to meet them. This understanding will not only enable the caregiver to provide a safe and calm experience that enhances global development of the children in her care, but also give parents realistic expectations of their child. This information will help adults give their children practical choices and enable the child to become responsible for their own behaviour.

Scenario 1

Three two-and-a-half-year-old girls are gathered in the doll corner at daycare, playing house. One of the three girls has already designated the roles that the other girls will play. Let's name the girls. Sally tells the others that she will be the "mommy," Judy will be the "big sister," and Allie will be "the baby." The girls are happy with their assigned roles, but then another girl, Jessie, comes to the center and wants to join in the play. Sally tells her that there is no room for her (even though the center is designed for four children). Jessie stands her ground, however, and tells Sally that *she* will be the "mommy"!

Of course, this does not go over well and an argument ensues. Their voices get louder as both girls pull at the same doll.

These are the choices:

 a. Close the center to the girls.

 b. Remove the two girls that are behaving inappropriately and separate them.

 c. Quickly assess the situation and ask the girls for their ideas, so that all of them can play happily. The educator acts as a moderator here, ensuring that all ideas are equally discussed and that all the children are able to come to a positive and productive solution.

Consequences of your decision:

 a. If the center is closed, what do the children learn? The two girls that were not part of the altercation suffer from a lack of valuable play time. It is true that they see a consequence of fighting or not playing respectfully, but now they do not learn how to work out differences with others. They also do not get to experience sharing and learn important negotiation skills that will need as they development into adults.

b. Again, if just the two fighting children are removed, the other girls still have valuable play time, but miss out on practicing their socializing and negotiation skills. This choice does not give any alternatives to the children who have witnessed this antisocial behaviour, and could potentially promote submissive and apathetic behaviour.

Children at all ages learn from their role models. They experiment with behaviours by imitating what they see. Very often, children do not see the consequences of various behaviours, or they are simply unable to decipher cause-and-effect relationships. It is imperative for the adult to guide them age-appropriately so that they can see the consequences.

Therefore, the two girls who were asked to leave will now know why they are experiencing this consequence of their actions. If they are put into a time-out, they will learn nothing, and autonomy is not promoted. Decision-making is also taken away, and with it, so is the child's personal responsibility for their behaviour. All these skills are developed using the first-choice strategy.

c. The only choice for the educator that can promote more positive social behaviour, is if the children are given respect, a feeling of security, and alternatives to their negative behaviours. This involves the educator allowing the children to talk about the incident, discuss the negative behaviours, and then help both girls to find solutions so that everyone's needs are met. This method turns a negative experience into a positive learning one. With a little repetition, so that all the children in the classroom can experience the lesson, the antisocial behaviour will should disappear.

Scenario 2

Your child has a playdate at your house. The children are in the same class at daycare, and you are friendly with the parents. The child arrives with her mother. They have been over many times before. Then, the children go to the play area, where all of your child's toys are displayed, and they begin to play.

They are sharing, talking, and deciding which toys to play with. You are talking with your friend close by (within sight and sound of the children). After 30 minutes, you go to the girls and tell them it's time for a snack, and that it's also time to cleanup. The girls do as they're told, and during this time, you notice the friend taking some small toys and putting them in her pocket. Your daughter does not see this.

These are the choices:

   a. Ignore the behaviour and just replace the toys as soon as possible.

   b. Immediately tell the child in a harsh tone of voice to put back the toys in front of your child.

   c. Go over discreetly to the child, and gently ask her to put the toys back.

Consequences of your decision:

   a. This might seem like the most straightforward solution, since it is not your child who has acted out and you may feel that it is not your job to confront your friend's child. This choice allows no learning, however, and might even encourage the other child to take someone's toys again. This also may leave you feeling uncomfortable about having another playdate.

b. This choice can be very embarrassing for both your child and her friend. When the environment becomes tense, not much learning can be accomplished. Your child might get very upset, and then everyone's friendship is jeopardized, including your friendship with the friend's mother.

c. When you approach the child discreetly, you can be successful in not only retrieving the toys, but also helping the little girl become responsible for her actions. Recognizing her mistake, she can now fix it with your help. In this scenario, you become a gentle role model that the child can learn from.

If you're comfortable, however, you may want to encourage a discussion about cleaning up toys in general, and putting everything back in its proper place. Organizational skills are very important to a child's development. When children are shown that toys have a "special place" where they go, they can internalize that knowledge and become more secure and confident about the routine.

You must also acknowledge that this behaviour is very age appropriate, and that the action is not indicative of a negative characteristic trait of the child.

You may also tactfully tell your friend, the child's mother, about the incident. Tread with extreme caution, however, as most parents do not like to hear anything negative about their child, especially from a friend.

Tip: When having a friend come over to play, you and your child should separate the toys that are for sharing, and those that are not. The children must also be told the toy limits (your child is included, as she may have forgotten!) before the play starts.

Adults should also be involved in the cleanup. Children at this age are not usually very excited to tidy up, and firm encouragement and guidance should be provided. Since they also don't possess a long attention span, adults should help them stay focused on their task.

Ages 3 years to 4 years:

A child this age is usually full of curiosity about everything in their environment. We often hear them ask "Why?" over and over again, not always waiting for a full explanation or answer. Every day is a day to explore and experience life, and therefore, learning is ongoing and constant as the child develops.

The adult's role for this age group should be one that allows the child to grow at their own personal rate in a safe and stimulating environment. Teachers and parents are extremely important when it comes to the healthy development of the child. Since the child is very aware of everything around them now, they process all that they see and hear. They also tend to imitate and repeat words and phrases at will. This is a natural and necessary way to help in their development, so that the child can navigate, explore and learn about their world.

The adult must ensure that this world is not only physically safe, but emotionally, also. Children of this age are eager to learn, explore, and experiment in new situations. Adults must encourage this natural inclination with positive reinforcement. Every mistake should be a learning experience, and every challenge an incentive to try again.

At this age, the child is developing and showing some impulse control. She reacts to stimulus with thought and meaning. She is also beginning to understand the feelings of others and she has an effect on not only other people, but on the things around her as well. She can be fascinated by how high she can build a tower, the mixing of colours, or just the texture of sand running through her fingers!

Physically, she is able to catch a ball, run backwards, hop on one foot, balance on one leg for a few minutes, peddle a tricycle, and know that she is meant to wear a helmet. She is also aware of rules, and loves to play games with rules (especially when she makes them up!). She is beginning to draw pictures with realistic detail, and can tell stories, both real and imaginative.

Her brain is making connections that will enable her to stimulate her memories, and eventually, learn academic skills. This age group is aware of their limitations and can compare themselves to others. Friendships are important, but are not necessarily solid. They are in a state of an emotional and social awakening. Knowing this, it is imperative that the important adults in this child's life are supportive and caring, while encouraging autonomy, problem-solving, and decision-making.

Scenario 1

Billy and Sammy are in the block area at daycare, building towers and playing an imaginary game of castles and dungeons. Jimmy comes up to them and sits down, almost breaking a tower. Sammy gets very angry and yells at Jimmy, calling him a baby. Jimmy yells that he is not a baby, and tells Sammy that *he* is the baby, and that his tower is not strong and that he will make a better one!

This makes Sammy very angry. He grabs Billy and tells him that they are going to the sandbox. Billy does not want to go, but feels compelled to follow him. Billy tries to tell Sammy that he wants to play with the blocks and with Jimmy. Sammy shouts and disturbs the class, screaming that they are *all* babies. This is not the first time that Sammy has shouted out in class, calling the other children names. His mother has told the teacher that at home he and his older brother get into many screaming fights.

These are the choices:

    a. Immediately go to Sammy and tell him to be quiet, since he is disturbing his friends in the class.

    b. Go to Billy and encourage him to return to the blocks with Jimmy.

    c. Settle the class down by doing a deep-breathing transition break, and then tell Sammy to choose another activity center himself.

Consequences of your decision:

    a. While Sammy is exhibiting this out-of-control behaviour, he will not be able to calm himself down and be quiet. He needs direction and a reminder that he is not going to be punished. He also needs to get control of his emotions, and as the educator, you can guide him to express his feelings in a socially acceptable way.

b. By suggesting to Sammy that he needs to remove himself from the situation, it gives him the respect that he needs to feel acknowledged that his feelings were hurt. It also allows him the break that he needs to become calm.

c. By encouraging Billy and Jimmy, you're respecting Billy's feelings and acknowledging that he also wants to play.

In this situation, a combination of all the choices can be effective, as each one addresses a different experience and behavior very often seen at this age.

Ages 4 years to 5 years:

This is the age when we see a great jump in all areas of development. Children are able to express their feelings and thoughts, not only through verbal language, but also through fine art. They have become very effective storytellers, dramatic actors, organizers of activities, and game players. They have their own sense of humor, and love listening to and telling jokes. Empathy towards others is also beginning to develop. They are beginning to show sympathy, not only for those they know, but also for strangers.

At this age, we see a conscious and moral judgment start to develop in the child, and this new understanding of the world around them can affect their thoughts, self-esteem and concept of self. Because of this developing awareness, a child can become very sensitive, not only with others around them, but in situations where they can interpret the social nuances of the environment as well.

As we see their cognitive development and thought processes rapidly progress, it is essential that we remember to have realistic expectations of these children in our care. They are still very fragile in their feelings about themselves, and therefore, it is imperative that the caregiver understands the child's capabilities and is able to encourage the child to grow and develop in a safe and positive environment.

A four-year-old enjoys playing games and usually follows the rules. At times, she enjoys making up games with her *own* rules! Physically, these children are able to run, jump, skip, dance and play organized, age-appropriate sports. They are also flexible, and they should be moving their bodies as much as possible. They can ride a tricycle or a four-wheel bike. They can catch and throw a ball, ski, skate, swim and participate in all outdoor and indoor activities with proper adult guidance. They should also be part of the decision as to which activities they want to participate in.

Scenario 1

The children in the pre-kindergarten class are playing age-appropriate baseball outside the daycare. There are 14 boys and girls who know the rules of the game as it is played. There are also two teachers who are supervising the game. All the children are participating and having fun.

Suddenly, two children begin fighting in the outer field. One child is screaming at the other, calling her a baby for

Scenarios

not being able to catch the ball. She responds that he had pushed her away from the ball and made her drop it. By this time, the teachers are on the scene and the game is paused. The children gather around, and some even start to join in the fight while others become very upset with this fighting and just want to get away. The teachers must quickly resolve the conflict and settle the children.

These are the choices:

    a. The teachers stop the game and send all the children to sit at the edge of the park in a time-out.

    b. One teacher takes the fighting children aside and the other teacher organizes for the rest of the children to continue the game.

    c. Both teachers question the two children who are angry, and have all the other children listen in. The teachers then encourage the two children to negotiate a resolution to the problem. During this process, the children that weren't involved or aren't interested in participating are invited to play in a different area of the park. One teacher accompanies these children.

Consequences of your decision:

    a. This time-out allows the children to be away from the altercation, but they do not learn any social behaviours or resolution skills. The children that were not involved are also being punished for no reason, and their feelings are being disrespected while their positive behaviours are not being acknowledged. They are just a nonentity part of a group.

    b. This choice reassures those children that didn't show negative social behaviour, but at the same time, they are not part of the learning process, which helps build negotiation skills. They are also are not involved in the resolution. They aren't given a choice as to their involvement in the process, and they are immediately directed away. This choice does give the teacher a smaller group to work with and find a resolution to this situation, however.

    c. Although it can be difficult for the teachers, this strategy of involving all the children gives them the opportunity to be a part of the negotiation process. With this approach, they can learn how to resolve an argument. Some children are given a choice as to their level of involvement, and therefore, their needs and feelings are being respected.

The children that are directly involved in this antisocial behaviour are participating in resolving their own conflict. Under the guidance of the teacher, they're learning how to have respect for others by practicing good listening skills, and are challenged to think of a fair outcome that will satisfy the needs of each child.

They also must show empathy towards each other and recognize that everyone is equal. This choice promotes development in the social, emotional, and cognitive domains. All children feel important now since their thoughts and feelings are being acknowledged. They are also given the opportunity to learn conflict resolution skills, because they are expected to come up with thoughtful strategies that incorporate empathy and respect for others.

Scenario 2

Anna is four years old and plays alone most of the time. The teachers have noticed that at the painting easel, she will start a painting but often rip her picture up and throw it away. She avoids confrontation at all times, and will give up her place, toy, or book as soon as some other child approaches her to share.

During cleanup, she puts the toys away, but insists that they must be back in their exact place. Everything must be in order, and if there is any sort of unexpected interruption, she gets very anxious and finds a place for herself away from everyone. As usual, after snack time, the children get ready to go outside. It is a winter day and they must wear boots and snow pants with their jackets, hats, and mittens. The teacher notices that Anna is very distraught in the locker room. Her clothes are in a messy ball and there is no sign of her boots. There is a pair of boots in another girl's locker, however. All the children are in the class getting dressed when the teacher realizes that another child has the wrong boots on! Anna doesn't move from the floor in front of her locker. What should the teacher do?

These are the choices:

  a. Go to Anna and quickly pick up her snowsuit, while telling her she is acting silly and that she should just get dressed, since she is holding up the class.

  b. Go to Anna and ask her open-ended questions to find out what has happened, and make sure that her feelings were not hurt.

c. Go to Anna and explain that the rest of the children are getting ready, and that you've noticed that she is upset. As you are talking with her, ask her to help you gather her clothes to take to the class. Verbally recognize that she does not have her boots, but tell her you've noticed that there is another pair in the locker.

Then negotiate with her as to what to do with those boots, and gently encourage her, as the rightful owner of those boots, to go and get her boots back. Avoid speaking about the fact that she is just sitting there and not able to complete the task of dressing. If she is able to fulfill the task of getting her boots back, you should help the two girls talk about the mistake and how Anna's feelings might have been hurt.

Consequences of your decision:

a. Anna's feelings of low self-esteem are not addressed, but are reinforced. When the teacher gathers up the clothes and tells her that she is acting silly, Anna is given neither encouragement nor guidelines to help herself become autonomous and fix the problem herself.

b. The teacher is showing some empathy for Anna's feelings, but is not promoting strong self-worth or teaching her any skills to resolve the conflict and move past her fear of confrontation.

c. The teacher is showing empathy while still encouraging autonomy and conflict resolution. It's likely that the other child did not realize she had Anna's boots, and it is actually Anna's responsibility to approach her to get her boots back. It is imperative that the educator is aware of each child's personality, their strengths and weaknesses, in order to promote positive self-esteem to each child effectively, so that everyone feels secure to make and fix mistakes.

Summary

5 steps to remember for the successful implementation of this strategy:

1. Offer only age-appropriate choices that are relevant to the situation, but also easy for the child to understand.

2. Encourage the child to make their own decision.

3. Enthusiastically reinforce the child's decision.

4. Praise the child as often as possible.

5. Remember that praise must be honest and meaningful.

Conclusion

This book is a compilation of research into various learning theorists, behaviour strategists, and child developmental researchers. From the research that focuses on the common behaviours children exhibit not only in social settings but also at the home, I have developed my own strategy that not only promotes child development in all areas of child growth, but also promotes socially acceptable behaviours. My personal experience as a teacher, educator, mother, grandmother, and professor has also helped form the foundation for my strategy.

The previous scenarios were created to show how the strategy of first observing the child's behaviour and then giving them different relevant choices often helps resolve the various behavioural issues. When using this theory, children learn that they are responsible for their own behaviour. We are also showing our children respect, and in turn, our children will return that respect, not only to family and other adults, but also to siblings and other people in their life.

We do not live alone on an isolated island where other people aren't involved in our day-to-day living. Our surroundings not only influence some of our thoughts, behaviours, and values, but also affect our judgements and successes. We are a community that must work together, learn together, and live together. A lot of recent research is showing that children need to build skills to be team players, while still keeping their independent thoughts. Respecting other people, animals, and our environment are also crucial lessons they must be taught.

This strategy is based on children feeling important and respected in their families and classrooms. This method of discipline teaches children that they alone are responsible for their behaviour. The adult is very important in the child's life, and if there are multiple adults, then it is very helpful that they share common goals, skills and strategies, as adult guidance is needed to achieve this important skill of personal responsibly. Infants are very dependent upon a caring adult for all their needs, but all children of all ages, also need to feel love, protection, strong self-esteem and respect from a nurturing adult. These feelings are fulfilled when they are transferred through the attention and genuine love of the parent/caregiver. The primary need of genuine attention must be fulfilled in order for a child to develop into a happy, productive adult.

The information in this handbook comes from personal observations and specific experiences I have been involved in. Through my teaching career, I have been exposed to the many philosophies of education, learning, and development theorists. I have formed my own opinions, however, using specific elements of these various strategies.

Using this strategy allows both the parent and childcare provider the flexibility to address each situation individually and uniquely. When the adult listens to the child and respects her needs, together they can find solutions to adapt unsociable behaviours into productive and positive ones.

When children receive positive attention, they will strive to keep this attention. Self-esteem and self-worth will be strengthened, and they will be able to accept challenges. As children develop, they will constantly be faced with decision-making. "The Choice Strategy," when applied often and consistently, develops the child's decision-making skills, enabling her to mature into a successful adult.

Happy Guiding!

About the Author

Jacquie Kaufman's career in early childhood education spans over forty years. A graduate from both Concordia University and Ottawa University, Jacquie has worked with schools, daycares and parents to enhance the quality of care and instruction given to preschool age children. Currently a college professor in child studies, she also regularly presents workshops to parents, daycare educators, and educational associations.

A mother of three successful adult children herself, Jacquie resides in Montreal. *I Am Not Happy with Your Behaviour!* is her first book.

www.ingramcontent.com/pod-product-compliance
Lightning Source LLC
Chambersburg PA
CBHW020915080526
44589CB00011B/607